The
Red  Hat
Guide to MANCHESTER
CITY CENTRE

by

K.C. Dowling

Grosvenor House
Publishing Limited

The right of K.C. Dowling to be identified as the author of this
work has been asserted in accordance with Section 78
of the Copyright, Designs and Patents Act 1988

Edited by Elaine McLean
Photographs by Ken Pilkington and Elaine McLean
Cover Design and illustration by Dianne Pilkington
Map Design and illustration by Beckie Wylie Rothwell

Woolworths Fire, Photo by kind permission of
Greater Manchester Fire Service Museum

This book is published by
Grosvenor House Publishing Ltd
28-30 High Street, Guildford, Surrey, GU1 3EL.
www.grosvenorhousepublishing.co.uk

A CIP record for this book
is available from the British Library

ISBN 978-1-78148-946-8

Revised Edition: August 2018

This book is dedicated to my first granddaughter, Rosa Grace Casey.

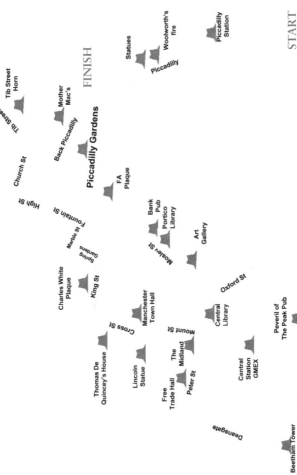

START

FINISH

Piccadilly Station

Woolworth's fire

Statues

Piccadilly

Tib Street Horn

Tib Street

Mother Mac's

Church St

Back Piccadilly

Piccadilly Gardens

High St

Fountain St

FA Plaque

Marble St

Spring Gardens

Bank Pub

Portico Library

Charles White Plaque

King St

Mosley St

Art Gallery

Cross St

Manchester Town Hall

Oxford St

Thomas De Quincey's House

Lincoln Statue

Mount St

Central Library

The Midland

Peter St

Central Station GMEX

Peveril of The Peak Pub

Free Trade Hall

Deansgate

Beetham Tower

The Briton's Protection

By the same author:

A Man of Insignificance   The Looked After Child
ISBN 978-1-78148-326-8   ISBN 978-1-78623-994-5

Contents

Manchester
Yesterday and Today

I was born and grew up in Manchester in the 1950s, 60s and 70s.

I crossed the city back and forth, almost every week-day on my way to school and later on in life, I studied and worked inside its boundaries.

I think of both time and place with nostalgia, after all Manchester is my home town and there are surely few amongst us who do not recall our home town with fondness.

For almost two thousand years, since Roman times, throughout most of its history, Manchester had been little more than a developing village. However, in the late 1700s, Manchester was thrust head-first into the forefront of the Industrial Revolution. This major historical period transformed Manchester's streets and buildings and gave its people the inimitable, unpretentious yet resolute, Mancunian character which they are renowned for. As with all dramatic change, there were some conflicting views concerning the consequences and outcomes of the period. Benjamin Disraeli said of Manchester in his political novel *Coningsby* (1844)

"Certainly Manchester is the most wonderful city of modern times."

In difference, the Victorian social thinker, John Ruskin, upon a visit to the city was so appalled at the air pollution that he notoriously and scathingly called Manchester "The Chimney of the World."

In the early 18th Century, Manchester had a population of around 10,000. By the end of that century the population had reached about 70,000. This was phenomenal growth by any standard.

It was in Manchester in the last century that scientists first split the atom and developed the stored programme computer.

Various *Clean Air Acts* in the 1950s and 1960s would at least have changed Ruskin's perception about Manchester's air quality, had he been around to see their impact. Nevertheless, even as a loyal Mancunian, I still remember the *city* of Manchester in the 1970s, as a grimy, backward looking place, which since being deposed as King of the industrial revolution, had, by the advent of the twentieth century, lost much of its vitality. By the arrival of the 1980s, the city centre in particular had become a scruffy, traffic congested scene, wherein Manchester had settled for, and established itself as, a dull, workaday town, in dire need of regeneration, in the grim 'up north,' of post-war Britain.

Not so today

Since the early 1990s, Manchester has undergone an unrecognizable transformation. Today's Manchester is a modern, glistening European destination of international importance.

Currently, Manchester is ranked as a *beta world city* by the *Globalization and World Cities Research Network*. It is the highest ranked British city after London. Ranked globally on a par with Montreal and Rio de Janeiro and above Belfast, Edinburgh, and Cardiff.

It is now renowned for being the economic hub of the UK's 'Northern Power House.' Manchester can also lay claim to: An International Airport where you can fly direct to Aberdeen or Abu Dhabi, Vienna or Vancouver; an innovative Metro link transport system admired the world over; two world famous football teams; noted musical exports and media links; a myriad of cosmopolitan bars and restaurants; definitely one and arguably two world-ranking universities; one of the largest undergraduate student communities in Europe; a culturally diverse population and much more besides.

This easy tour takes us on foot through Manchester City Centre. It is not strenuous and can be completed comfortably within a few hours. This includes the three pub stops, less time if you are abstemious.

We cannot hope to see all of Manchester in this time, much longer would be needed to accomplish this. The Red Hat Guide is not exhaustive, nor is it a lecture tour, nor is it intended as a serious, chronologically ordered, history lesson. You will not discover within its pages, tips on the best restaurants, the cheapest hotels, where the shops are, the number of the bus to take you to a specific destination, what shows are currently playing in town or the addresses of any resident celebrities. There is enough of this information to be found elsewhere and this guide does not seek to inform on any of that.

What you will see, during this walk will be some of the city's incredible statues and some of the magnificent buildings of Manchester. We will learn about some of the famous or infamous incidents that took place and we will hear about some of the sons, daughters and residents of, and visitors to, this city.

For the less earnest and more casual amongst us, this short journey can be thought of as a moderate stroll around one of today's world significant cities, hopefully in the famous 'Manchester sunshine,' with perhaps a few interesting distractions and stories along the way.

Marple

Our stroll really begins at Manchester Piccadilly Station.

However, before I arrive there, please permit me a distraction. I have a short, twenty-one minute train journey to make from Marple, which is where I live, so if you will kindly indulge me, I may as well tell you a little bit about the place which has now become my home. Marple is a small town which lies on the River Goyt. It is in the south east corner of Stockport which is now in the county of Greater Manchester and is about 12 miles from Manchester city centre. It has a population of around 23,000 and is also serviced by a series of canals. These canals once operated commercially but are now used exclusively for leisure.

Marple is also known for its high density of canal locks, there are 16 in all, known collectively as *Marple Lock Flight.*

Marple has two separate 'claims to fame,' both involving people, one a man the other a woman.

One was a significant, real historical figure, yet, he is hardly known at all outside Marple, whereas the other, although being a complete work of fiction and the subject of somebody else's imagination, is renowned throughout the world.

The first one is John Bradshaw who was born in Marple of farming stock. In 1649, Bradshaw was the judge who presided over the trial of King Charles I. During the trial he wore a bullet-proof hat and armour under his judge's robes. He was the man who committed regicide by sentencing the 'Martyr' Monarch to death and described the English king in court as being, 'Tyrant, Traitor, Murderer, and a public enemy.' On January 31st 1661, after the restoration of Charles II, Bradshaw's body, together with the bodies of Oliver Cromwell and Henry Ireton was posthumously exhumed, placed on display and eventually beheaded. His head was displayed on a pike at Westminster Hall as a deterrent to all who would ever consider such crimes again.

Marple's other claim concerns the author Agatha Christie (1890-1976). Agatha Christie is one of the best-selling writers of all time. Her writing is varied but she is famous mainly for her 66 detective novels and her 14 short story collections all of which she published in her lifetime. She has sold over 4 Billion books which have been translated into 56 different languages. She has also written 12 plays including "The Mousetrap," which is the longest running theatrical play in the world. It opened in 1952 starring a 29 year old Richard Attenborough and is still running now.

The story goes, that in the summer of 1925, Agatha Christie had devised a new character. She had thought everything out, but couldn't settle on a name for this character. Every name that came into her head, she quickly discarded for a variety of reasons. She was travelling by train to Manchester, to visit her brother-in-law, who lived in Abney Hall, in nearby Cheadle. The train engine suffered a mechanical failure. All the passengers had to disembark whilst the train operators tried to resolve the situation. As Agatha Christie sat on the platform in the summer sunshine, she nonchalantly glanced over at the name of the train station, which was of course – Marple, and she instantly had the name of her most famous character, the enduring, Jane Marple, or as she is better known, 'Miss Marple.' Miss Marple is an elderly spinster, amateur sleuth, who appears in twelve Agatha Christie books.

This caricature of Miss Marple drawn by an unknown artist as it appears on the wall at Marple Train Station.

Piccadilly Train Station

Manchester is truly the place where the railway age began for the whole world. It was the service established between Manchester and Liverpool which first demonstrated the use of rail as a viable public and freight transport system.

Manchester Piccadilly Station is the principal train station in Manchester.

The opening of Piccadilly Station in 1842, 'Store Street Station,' as it was then called, was a key achievement in the prosperity of Manchester. The main feature of the station was that it made direct travel from Manchester to London possible in just under ten hours. The quickest method of travel between these two cities before the station opened was to undertake that journey by stagecoach which unreliably took around twenty-four hours and could be a very uncomfortable, even hazardous excursion. As well as this and much more importantly, for the sake of commerce, the stagecoach had obvious freight restrictions. If you decide to carry more cargo by train, then you just put another carriage on. You couldn't do this with a team of horses. Rail link together with the canal system established Manchester's industrial base as a powerhouse city in the 19th Century.

In 1847, the station was re-named 'London Road' and in 1960 it was again re-named 'Piccadilly.'

In 1998, Piccadilly Station was extensively refurbished. It had a slate roof and as a consequence was very dark inside. The slate was replaced with over 10,000 panes of special glass. This glass is very thin and carries a risk of fracture. To protect the public from any fragment fall, a netting system has been installed as a safety precaution. If you look carefully at the station ceiling you will be able to see the netting and the glass.

At a cost of £100M the station was refurbished again in 2002. During this refurbishment, Piccadilly Station, was made more leisure and consumer friendly with the addition of cafes, bars, coffee shops and retail outlets. Today, if you wished you could probably do your weekly shop there.

With a touch of irony for the people of Manchester, the name 'Piccadilly' originally comes from London and has its source in a London tailor who had a shop there, from where he sold 'picadils,' a form of stiff collar in the 1600s.

Piccadilly Station handles around 25 million passenger exits and entries every year and is one of the busiest train stations in the U.K. As well as a tram and train interchange, it also acts as a meeting place for many travellers.

The outcome of a survey conducted in 2007 saw Piccadilly Station emerge with the highest level of customer satisfaction for any train station in the UK. Ninety-two per cent of passengers expressed satisfaction with the station compared to a 60% average at other stations throughout the UK.

At the time of writing it has recently been announced that Piccadilly Station is to undergo yet another expansion programme. This is part of the planned Northern Hub, the objective of which is to improve the transport infrastructure of Manchester. Plans are well in advance for this ambitious development which also includes Oxford Road Station which is about half a mile from Piccadilly. The estimated cost for this programme is a staggering £1 billion.

Piccadilly

As we leave Piccadilly Station and walk down Piccadilly Approach, it is now lined by shops on one side and hotels on the other. Most of these buildings started life as cotton warehouses in the 1800s. If you look over to the building that is currently the Malmaison Hotel you will see the well preserved terracotta plaque for Joshua Hoyle & Sons, an eminent cotton merchant. In 1853, at the height of what was known as *Cottonopolis* there were 108 cotton mills in Manchester.

In 1879, the first telephone exchange outside the USA was opened in nearby Faulkner Street. The whole network had only 125 subscribers. Five soundproofed phone boxes were placed in the building. They were apparently in constant use with queues forming to use them.

Who were these users calling?

Piccadilly Gardens

The location was originally one of disused water filled clay pits.

In 1755 Manchester Royal Infirmary was built there and remained until 1914. Next door to it, stood the 'Lunatic Asylum.'

Shortly after World War One, the site was transformed to Piccadilly Gardens and remained as such throughout the 1900s. In 2002 the site was revamped again to what you see today. For reasons unknown it is considered by many Mancunians to be the centre of the city.

Piccadilly Statues

There are four magnificent statues in Piccadilly.

Duke of Wellington by Mathew Noble, unveiled in 1856.

Duke of Wellington

Poet Laureate, Alfred Lord Tennyson hailed him as the 'last great Englishman.' Born Arthur *Wesley* later changed to *Wellesley*. It seems to be a convenient bout of memory loss for the whole English nation that the man who is still acclaimed to be one of the greatest Englishman of all time is actually a born and bred Irishman.

Born in Dublin in 1769 and raised in Summerhill, County Meath. He had a distinguished military and political career, achieving the highest office in both, but he is undoubtedly best known for his defeat of Napoleon Bonaparte at the battle of Waterloo in 1815.

This statue is a substantial figure; Wellington stands on a stone pillar and seated beneath him are four allegoricals, three female and one male. They are made in the highly ornate and extravagant style of baroque and are symbolic of War, Wisdom, Peace and Victory. The four panels below the allegoricals depict scenes from Wellington's career. They include two battle scenes, the one at Waterloo and another one in India. The other two depict him in civic society, one of which is a House of Commons scene. The monument as a whole is designed to be walked around so that different perspectives can be gained.

Queen Victoria by Edward Onslow Ford, unveiled 1901.

Queen Victoria

Born in 1819, as Alexandrina Victoria Saxe Coburg Saalfield, Queen Victoria came via a circuitous inheritance route to the throne of the United Kingdom and Ireland.

Under normal circumstances she wouldn't have got a look in and would have been considered a minor royal, but these were not normal circumstances. Her own father was Prince Edward, fourth son of George III. Both he and George III, died in 1820. Then each of the older royal brothers died in turn, none of them leaving any legitimate heir. By the time she was 18 years old, she was Queen.

As Queen Victoria she was Britain's longest reigning monarch, (1837 – 1901). Elizabeth II overtook her on September 9th 2015. Victoria herself had 9 children with her husband Prince Albert. Many of them married into the royal families of Europe. She was said to be the Royal Grandmother of Europe. The Victorian era in Britain is viewed by many historians as the greatest era of all.

This statue of her is a large, bronze, over life size, seated figure of the monarch. The main message seemingly, is to convey motherhood. An obviously older monarch the sculptor makes no attempt to disguise this, yet the figure has presence and dignity. It was unveiled in 1901 by sculpture Edward Onslow Ford.

Robert Peel by William Calder Marshall, unveiled 1853.

Robert Peel

Robert Peel (1788 – 1850) was born in nearby Bury, Lancashire. The son of a wealthy textile merchant. He was educated at Harrow public school and then Oxford University, where he studied Classics and Mathematics, graduating with a double first honours degree.

After leaving Oxford and probably as a result of his father's influence and connections, he first entered Parliament as the MP for Cashel, Tipperary, Ireland, at the age of twenty-one. Cashel was classified as a 'rotten borough.' It contained only 24 electors and the young Peel was elected unopposed.

He held many high offices of the day, including two terms as Home Secretary. He also had two separate terms as British Prime Minister. Although he has been accredited with much in civic life, he is probably best known as the inventor of the modern police force. In an indirect tribute to this, in England, police officers are often known as *Bobbies* and in Ireland as *Peelers*.

He had seven children, some of whom gained distinction in their own right. One of them, William Peel was a recipient of the Victoria Cross.

Robert Peel died as a result of falling from his horse in the summer of 1850.

James Watt by William Theed, unveiled 1857.

James Watt

James Watt (1736 – 1819) was born into a prosperous middle-class family in Glasgow, Scotland. Their fortunes would decline before Watt became a young man. He was an inventor and a Mechanical Engineer.

He is accredited by many as being the ingenious engineering power behind the industrial revolution. It is said that he took civilization from... 'farm house to factory.'

He did not invent the steam engine, but he modernised it and his modernisation is accredited with driving the industrial revolution. Manchester adopted many of his inventions. He calculated that a solitary horse could pull 180 lbs in weight and he called that '... one horse power'... He also gave his name to a unit of electricity... the Watt.

For those of us with an engineer's mind, Watt's great invention was the realisation that he could make the standard steam engine more efficient by using a separate chamber to condense steam without cooling the rest of the engine.

The statue is made of bronze and sits on a granite pedestal. It is by the English sculptor, William Theed and was unveiled in 1857. This dynamic Glaswegian is portrayed as a solitary, pensive figure, holding a technical instrument and a sheaf of papers.

Mosley Street

Mosley Street, was the first *posh* street in Manchester and takes its name from a prominent family of the time. The nearby streets were laid out in late 1700s and were the centre of the fashionable part of town.

At the junction of Mosley Street and Market Street is a building that is currently used for retail purposes but for much of the 1800s, was The Royal Hotel. It is well known for being the premises where the first ever train travel ticket in the world was purchased. It is though better known for the following. On 17th April 1888, a group of men met here. Their leaders were J.J. Bentley from Bolton and William McGregor from Birmingham. By the time the meeting rose, the modern Football Association (F.A.) had been founded.

There is a plaque to commemorate this occasion although for ease of reading the plaque fixers could have sited it a bit lower. You may be surprised to learn that on that day there were none of today's football giants; Chelsea, Liverpool, Arsenal and in particular the two Manchester clubs, United and City were for a variety of reasons, all conspicuous by their absence.

Representatives who attended on that day were from the following clubs; Accrington Stanley, Aston Villa, Blackburn Rovers, Bolton Wanderers, Burnley, Derby, Everton, Notts County, Preston North End, Stoke, West Brom and Wolverhampton. These clubs were the founders of modern day football.

The first season commenced in the autumn of 1888 and concluded in the spring of 1889. Preston came out as league champions and were undefeated throughout the whole season. Their top scorer was John Goodall who scored 21 goals in 21 matches, a ratio that today would be priceless.

The Bank Pub:
Portico Library

As we walk further down Mosley Street, on the left hand side, we will come upon a pub called 'The Bank.' This whole building was originally the Portico Library and was purpose built in 1803 by a group of Manchester and Liverpool businessmen. The Portico

Library was the first subscription library in Manchester. It was designed by Thomas Harrison, the same architect who built the Liverpool Lyceum. The facade is based on the Temple of Athens Palais, even though Harrison in his lifetime didn't once set foot in Greece.

The world renowned Manchester Literature and Philosophical Society (Lit & Phil) regularly met there. The first Chairperson of The Portico Library was the Reverend William Gaskell who was the incumbent Unitarian Minister at nearby Cross Street Chapel. Gaskell was a poet in his own right, but his literary endeavours were eclipsed by those of his own wife, the acclaimed writer Elizabeth Cleghorn Gaskell; amongst her works are *Cranford, North and South* and *Mary Barton*, all of which are still in print today.

The first Secretary of The Portico Library was Peter Mark Roget, the son of a Swiss clergyman. Roget studied medicine at Edinburgh University and graduated in 1798. His life seemed to be punctuated by tragic incidents. One of which concerned his favoured uncle Samuel Romilley, an eminent lawyer. On the death of his wife in1818, Romilley shut himself away in his house in Russell Square, London and took to his bed. In the grip of delirium he leapt from his bed and slit his own throat with an open razor. He survived his suicidal action for little more than an hour. Roget was actually in attendance at his uncle's house when this incident occurred.

Although a qualified physician he spent little of his life practising. He did though as a young doctor publish a paper on *Tuberculosis* and another one on the effects of *Laughing Gas* which was then widely used as an anaesthetic. He also invented a slide rule that was commonly used in schools and universities before the advent of the calculator. He is most famous for publishing the first Thesaurus. His name is synonymous with this book which is now universally known as *Roget's Thesaurus*. When it was first published in 1852, its content was acclaimed, but its title was condemned for being too long, it was:

"Thesaurus of English Words and Phrases Classified and Arranged so as to Facilitate the Expression of Ideas and Assist in Literary Composition."

Roget lived until he was 90 years old.

Manchester Art Gallery

Barely 100 metres after The Bank Pub is Manchester Art Gallery. The Gallery is a publicly owned art museum that has around 500,000 visitors each year. It is actually three originally separate buildings that are interconnected and dates from 1824. It is a Grade 1 listed building; Manchester has 15 Grade 1 listed buildings. Currently, admission to the Gallery is free and it is open 7 days a week.

There is nowhere in England outside London that can match the breadth and quality of the exhibits in this Art Gallery. It contains 2000 oil paintings and 3000 water colours. Pictures by such artists as Turner, Chagall, Modigliani and many more. There is a vibrant collection of Victorian art and strong representation by the pre-Raphaelite Brotherhood.

One artist who is strongly represented is French born artist Pierre Adolphe Valette. For reasons which seem to be unknown, Valette visited Manchester in 1904. It became his adopted home and he lived and taught in the city. One of his most famous pupils was Laurence Stephen (L.S.) Lowry, a painter from humble beginnings who was born and lived locally and now receives world acclaim for his work which sells around the world for record prices.

A lesser known record held by L.S. Lowry is the one that he holds for turning down the most offers of civic honours in the U.K. Between 1955 and 1976 he rejected no less than 5 separate honours including a knighthood in 1968. He never really discussed the reasons for his refusal apart from telling his friend, fellow local artist Harold Riley that *he didn't want to change his situation.*

The relationship between politicians and artistes has always been an uneasy one. In this respect Manchester is no different than anywhere else inasmuch as there has always been a group of politicians who would sell the city's art treasures on and use the money to mend the potholes in the road. Conversely there has always been a group of artistes who would use all the city's money for buying the most outlandish pieces of art whilst all around them were homeless and starving. The artistes accuse the politicians of being *philistines* and the politicians accuse the artistes of being *artistes*. There is the story of one Manchester City mayor who when addressing an audience at a gallery function, proudly pointed at the paintings around the room and said,

"None of your manufactured stuff 'ere, real masterpieces these and all 'and painted.'

Amongst the unique paintings that are in almost permanent residence in the gallery are;

A Moor by James Northcote. This was the first ever picture acquired by the gallery.

The Sirens and Ulysses by William Etty.

The Hireling Shepherd by William Holman Hunt

The Scapegoat by William Holman Hunt

Sappho by Charles Mengin

Work by Ford Maddox Brown

Valette has a room in the gallery exclusively dedicated to his work. This exhibition contains several of his contemporaneous urban landscapes of Manchester. The best known is probably: *Albert Square, Manchester*, painted in 1910.

Central Library

Before 1850, there were no such things in the U.K. as free public lending libraries. If you wanted a book then you had to buy it, borrow it from someone or find another way. There were libraries, but they were privately financed and ordinary people couldn't afford the subscriptions. In 1850 the government passed the Public Libraries and Museums Act, and shortly after, the first ever significant free lending library was opened in…. Manchester.

When Manchester actually opened the library in 1852 there was tremendous national interest in its success. Charles Dickens, the writer, attended the opening ceremony. The library didn't have any books, so the Mayor set up a public subscription fund. In a short time he had raised £12,000, the equivalent of £1/2Million in today's money. Every ten years the number of books outgrew the building and the library was constantly moving to a new address to accommodate them. By the mid 1920s it was decided that a new library was needed. In 1930 the architect E Vincent Harris was commissioned. The foundation stone was laid by Prime Minister, Ramsay McDonald and the new library was officially opened by King George V, in 1934.

A columned portico connected to a rotunda domed structure, the design was inspired by The Pantheon in Rome and its neo classical lines can often give the impression that it is much older than it is. When it was opened it was the largest free lending library in the country.

Manchester Central Library can boast some famous members and readers.

The writer Anthony Burgess was a regular visitor here as a young student. English folk singer Ewan McColl spent many hours and days 'keeping warm' inside its walls. Tony Warren, the creator of the longest running television programme in the world, *Coronation Street*, is said to have played truant there as a schoolboy.

Pubs:
Peveril of The Peak
& Britons Protection

Peveril of The Peak is one of the oldest surviving pubs in Manchester. It is said to date back to 1829. It is a Grade 11 listed building which was named after a famous stagecoach which used to run from London to Manchester in the early 1800s. The stagecoach in turn was named after *Peveril of The Peak*: a novel by

Sir Walter Scott published in 1823. The novel itself is Scott's longest novel and is considered to be one of his *English novels*, together with his works; *Ivanhoe, Woodstock and Kenilworth. Peveril of the Peak* is set against the background of a "Popish Plot" to assassinate King Charles II and replace him on the throne with his Catholic brother James.

During 1995 the pub was used to film episodes of the TV detective series *Cracker.*

One of Manchester's original drinking 'dens,' this pub prides itself on its traditional status and everything about it says that it intends to stay that way. The outside of the pub is painted and tiled in two glorious shades of pea green soup. Allegedly amongst its past regulars have been; Eric Cantona, the ex -Manchester United foot- baller, actors; Robbie Coltrane, Christopher Ecclestone, Ian McShane, John Thaw and also world renowned architect Norman Foster.

During World War 2, the upstairs living quarters of the pub was allegedly used as a brothel by American G.I.s who were stationed over here.

'The Peveril' also has a paranormal resident. Some customers claim to have seen empty glassware actually levitate from the bar and into the glass washer. None of these customers though would testify as to whether they had witnessed this at the beginning of their drink session or at the end of it.

The Britons Protection

Again one of the oldest surviving pubs in Manchester. This pub stands at the junction of Great Bridgewater Street and Lower Mosley Street.

The Britons Protection is a Grade 11 listed building, said to date back to 1795, when it opened as 'The Ancient Briton.' There are several explanations for its name change, a popular one being that it gave comfort and shelter to some of the casualties in The Peterloo Massacre which took place on August 19th 1819.

It is particularly famous for the extensive collection of whiskey that it has for sale. There are apparently around 200 different varieties of whiskey on offer. Scotch, Irish, American et al.

Inside, in one of the bars, on the wall, is a mural which commemorates the 'Peterloo Massacre.' More about this tragic event, later on in the guide. This mural is the only such commemoration of its kind in Manchester and The Britons Protection is worth a visit, if for no other reason than this.

As one reviewer writes;

"This tardis like interior oozes Manchester history – you can imagine Henry Hunt and his supporters sipping their last ale or two in here back on that hot August day in 1819, before some of them were brutally killed outside".

Another story that exists (although un-evidenced) about the origin of the name, concerns the civil war (1642–1651) between the Royalists and the Parliamentarians. It is said that the site was the Regional Parliamentarian recruiting office and that anybody who signed up was doing so, to protect his country, hence ...Britons Protection.

Beetham Tower

Worthy of mention, if only because at 554 feet (169 Metres) it is the tallest building in Manchester. As you stand outside The Britons Protection pub its height completely dominates the landscape.

It is a mixed use skyscraper and was completed in 2006. Noted for its thinness, 'Beetham' has a floor space of 525,000 square feet. It cost £150M to build. In total there are 47 floors, the first 23 comprise the

Manchester Hilton Hotel, the remaining floors are apartments and penthouses. In windy weather the tower is said to emit an intermittent hum which can be heard over three hundred metres away. The noise has been said to have occasionally brought the production of 'Coronation Street', the longest running TV soap in the world, which is produced half a mile away and has been continuously on the air since 1960, to a temporary halt.

Beetham was designed by Rochdale born Architect, Ian Simpson. It is said, Mr Simpson occupies the top two floors as a penthouse and that he has built an olive and lemon grove garden up there and thus occupies the highest living space in the United Kingdom. This living space occupies 12,500 square ft.

Manchester from 23rd Floor

Central Station: GMex

Central Station was opened as a train station in 1880. It was designed and built by the renowned English born civil engineer Sir John Fowler. In 1853, Fowler became Chief Engineer of the Metropolitan Railway in London, the world's first underground railway. He also held a similar position with District Railway, also in London. He was famous the world over for his engineering projects but was probably most famous for his astronomical salary. For his work on the Metropolitan he was paid the sum of £152,000, which is around £12 million at today's valuation and for his work on the District Railway, he was paid a similar sum.

One Railway Chairman felt obliged to remark... 'No engineer in the world was ever so highly paid.'

Probably the most famous connection to this building is a notorious one and it is to the Manchester Moors Murderers: Ian Brady and Myra Hindley. Brady and Hindley murdered at least five children, from the Manchester area over a two year period in the 1960s. The murderers earned their name because some of the victim's bodies were found buried on Saddleworth Moor in nearby Oldham. Some commentators actually believe that the number of murder victims is actually higher.

Hindley died in prison in 2002. Brady died recently, (2017) detained in a secure mental hospital.

When detectives were investigating these atrocities they had Brady and Hindley marked out as prime suspects but they had no hard evidence. They had searched Brady's home several times but these searches had produced nothing. During the last search they found a bible and hidden in the spine of the book was a left luggage ticket which they traced to Central Station. When detectives opened the locker they found a small suitcase which contained transcripts and audio tape recordings of the tortures and murders as they had actually happened. These findings were crucial in bringing about Brady and Hindley's convictions.

The trial judge, Mr Justice Atkinson, described Brady and Hindley as, 'Two sadistic killers of the utmost depravity.'

The Free Trade Hall

The Free trade Hall was originally built by public subscription as a public meeting hall for the people of Manchester. Construction of it took three years and was completed in 1856. It was heavily bombed in World War 2, during the Manchester Christmas Blitz, an intensive two night bombing campaign which saw an estimated 684 people lose their lives and a further 2364 people injured. It was rebuilt after the war and re-opened in 1951 as Manchester's premier concert venue and home of the world famous Halle Orchestra. As well as being home to the Halle, it was also up until 1996 Manchester's premier concert venue for the world's top musicians/singers when they 'played' Manchester.

On the night of 17th May 1966, Bob Dylan was onstage. His concert was in two parts. The first part involved Dylan on stage alone, singing and accompanied by nothing else but his acoustic guitar. After the interval Dylan reappeared with his unannounced band, the all-electric 'Hawks.' The appearance of the Hawks together with the appearance of Dylan himself now holding an electric guitar, brought howls of derision from the audience, with one audience member shouting "Judas." This incident has gone down as an iconic moment in musical history.

It is currently being used as a hotel and the building contains the memorial plaque to the Peterloo Massacre.

The Peterloo Massacre

In August 1819, living and economic conditions were harsh in England and nowhere were the effects of these conditions felt more severely than Manchester. The area within the environs that now contain Manchester Town Hall, The Midland Hotel, Central Station and Lower Mosley Street and what was The Free Trade Hall, made up a croft in 1819. This croft was known as St Peter's Field.

On August 16th a demonstration and an oration was held in St Peter's Field. Some estimates put the attendance at 100,000. The magistrates, fearing a riot, called on the militia to arrest the leaders and disperse the crowd. The Militia, many of them drunk, charged at the crowd on horseback.

Members of the public were trampled, hacked at with sabres and shot at. The crowd was dispersed in less than ten minutes but in that time hundreds of people were injured and 15 were dead. Amongst the dead were a Battle of Waterloo veteran, a two year old child and a disabled woman who was pregnant. Probably because The Battle of Waterloo had taken place a few years earlier the incident was dubbed *The Peterloo Massacre*. The world looked on in shock and horror and it became a defining moment in the history of society. It also inspired the poet Percy Bysshe Shelley to write his poem, The *Masque of Anarchy.*

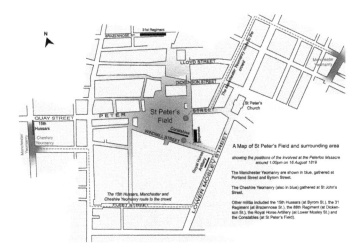

The map shows St Peter's Field and surrounding area.

Showing the positions of those involved around 1:00pm on the 16th August 1819.

The Manchester Yeomanry are shown gathered at Portland Street and Byrom Street.

The Cheshire Yeomanry are gathered at St John Street.

Other militia included the 15th Hussars (also at Byrom Street), the 31st Regiment at Brazennose Street, the 88th Regiment at Dickenson Street, the Royal Horse Artillery at Lower Mosley Street and the Constables at St Peter's Field.

Midland Hotel

Charles Trubshaw was an architect who prior to building the Midland Hotel had only ever built Railway Stations. It was therefore inevitable that some critics would say that the Midland Hotel looked like one and of course some of them did.

Commissioned by the Midland Railway Company in their failed expectancy of coming to Manchester, it opened in 1903. This grand Edwardian, 312 bedroom hotel is a Grade 2 listed building.

The hotel's guest list is so illustrious it is impossible to start it and completely out of the question to close it. Anybody who is anybody and has visited Manchester has stayed here and is still doing so.

Henry Edmunds, a distinguished member of the Automobile Club, arranged a historic meeting, between

Rolls Royce Commemorative Plaque in Midland Foyer.

Charles Stuart Rolls met Frederik Henry Royce. This meeting took place at the Midland Hotel on May 4th in 1904, whereupon the company of Rolls Royce was born.

The actual building itself contains much polished granite, terracotta and ceramics which were often selected because of their known resistance to smoke and soot, of which in Manchester in 1903, there would have been an abundance.

In the 1970s, Evelyn Waugh's, *Brideshead Revisited* was being filmed for television at Manchester's Granada Studios. The eminent acting cast and the executive production team were all staying at the Midland Hotel, amongst them were actors such as Jeremy Irons, Claire Bloom, John Gielgud and Sir Laurence Olivier. During the early hours of the morning the fire alarm went off. The producer of the show, raced frantically up and down the corridor trying to wake his actors and production staff. Despite repeated knocking on Gielgud's door, the aged thespian didn't respond in any way at all, and the producer waited for what seemed an age outside Olivier's room, who eventually appeared in his pyjamas blinking at the offender.

'What is it?' asked Olivier.

'Larry, Larry, there appears to be a fire!'

'Really? Oh, what awfully bad luck, do let me know if there is anything I can do,' came the reply, followed by a shutting door.

Town Hall

The original, irregular, triangular site housed the fire brigade and the corporation workshops in an area known as 'Town Yard.' The Town Hall building that now stands upon this site is regarded as one of the finest examples of Gothic revival architecture in the world. It is certainly one of the most magnificent town halls in England. It is a highly significant presence in the city and is obviously a Grade 1 listed building. The now pedestrianised area immediately surrounding it, was a traffic island until the mid-1980s.

Original construction began in 1868 and was completed in 1877 for a total expenditure of £859,000. The building remains a dynamic representation of civic pride and a most distinguished architectural work. It is said that the brief given to competing architects was to:

"Produce a work equal if not superior to any similar building in the country at any cost." This magnificent building was designed and built by the Liverpool born architect Alfred Waterhouse and is a tour all on its own. There was much criticism when Waterhouse was awarded the contract. Much was made of and said that in a previous building he had placed the female jury and witness room next to the gentleman's lavatory.

The Town Hall's Albert Square frontage is 323 feet (98m) and at its highest point it is 286 ft (87metres) high. The construction was comprised of 14 million bricks encased in Spinkwell Stone. The clock tower contains no less than 24 bells. The largest of them is one known as Great Abel, which weighs more than 8 tonnes and was named after the mayor of Manchester at that time, Abel Heywood.

Queen Victoria was asked to perform the opening ceremony but bluntly refused. No official reason for this snub was ever given but it was widely believed that she professed discomfort at having to be on the same platform as Heywood who had a radical background and who had been previously sent to prison for his seditious publishing.

The Manchester Bee

The Worker Bee was adopted by Manchester as a logo during The Industrial Revolution. Seven bees were included in the crest of the city's arms which were created in 1842. As you walk around the city centre you may notice the emblem. It appears on many things from buildings to bridges, from bollards to bins. The bee denotes the hard work ethic of the Mancunian.

Abraham Lincoln's Statue: Lincoln Square

There are only two statues of Abraham Lincoln in all of England. One is in Parliament Square in London, the other is in Lincoln Square, Manchester.

It is a bronze statue on a granite pedestal. The story of the statue's arrival at Lincoln Square is a convoluted one.

It begins in 1910 in Cincinnati, Ohio, USA, where-upon wealthy American businessman Charles Taft gave American sculptor George Grey Barnard a $100,000 commission to produce two statues of arguably, America's greatest President. One for Cincinnati and one for London. When Barnard's statue was eventually unveiled in 1917, it was met with much negative criticism. At the heart of this criticism was Barnard's presentation of Lincoln, who was depicted in shabby clothes, with a hunched frame, wearing a melancholic expression and with huge hands and feet. One critic said that Lincoln had the appearance of a 'dolt,' another said a 'tramp'. Another dubbed it the 'stomach ache statue.' This was mainly because of the depiction of the position of the hands. The Americans quickly recommissioned and sent a more traditional statue to London which now stands in Parliament Square: but what to do with this one?

After much deliberation it was decided that it should be hidden away in a provincial English city, but which one?

The first suggestion was Norwich, but no connection could be found between the late President Lincoln and this eastern, English city. Next up was Liverpool but this was also discarded, then finally Manchester was settled upon. The statue arrived in Manchester in 1919 and was met with the same critical controversy it had received in America. When asked why the statue had come to Manchester a spokesman for the Anglo American Society, John A Stewart, made up a story about Mancunian-American relations during the American civil war. It was completely untrue but it was a good speech and over the years his assertions came to be accepted as the truth. The real truth was that most Mancunians had never even heard of Abraham Lincoln and as well as this, opinion had been divided in Manchester regarding the American War with some Lancashire mills even flying their own American confederate flags during the struggle. Nevertheless, Stewart's comments passed into Manchester folklore and his words would find their way in inscription on the base of the statue. When Mancunians first saw the statue as it arrived on London Road train station platform, there was a move to give it back and it was stored in the nearby fire station at Whitworth Street, until The Anglo American Society could decide what to do with it. There was a suggestion that it should remain in the fire station out of sight. Eventually though it was erected in a corner in Platt Fields Park, which is a suburban park about 3 miles to the south of the city centre. There it remained relatively unseen and unheard of for over sixty years. In the mid 1980's Manchester City Council were developing the area. So they moved the statue into its present location and called the location, 'Lincoln Square.'

Dalton's Entry and Mulberry Passage

Although John Dalton (1766-1844) has a long association with Manchester he was born and raised in Eaglesfield, near Cockermouth, Cumberland. Despite coming from a poor Quaker family he received a private education through a philanthropic patron. By the time he was 13 years old he was working as a teacher himself and by the time he was 14 years old he was prolific in Latin. He had originally planned to study Medicine but as a religious dissenter he was automatically barred from entering any English Universities. As a young man he came to Manchester to teach Mathematics at the "New College," a dissenting academy.

He settled permanently in Manchester and is universally accepted as Manchester's first important scientist and is said to be "The Father of Modern Chemistry."

He particularly distinguished himself in the fields of: Atomic Theory, Meteorology and was one of the first scientists to recognise colour blindness, a condition that he suffered from himself.

Dalton was also a member of Manchester's renowned Literature and Philosophical Society "Lit & Phil" and was the author and presenter of many papers to its members.

Dalton was often to be found wandering around Manchester with various instruments taking readings of temperatures and wind pressures. He is said to have recorded over 200,000 weather, observations. Whatever the weather, he always carried with him, his trademark umbrella which he considered to be the 'sign of a gentleman.'

He left New College after being in post 8 years and thereafter earned his living teaching and lecturing.

When he died, there were 40,000 mourners at his funeral. The preservation of this ginnel, serves to commemorate John Dalton's association with the city.

Thomas De Quincey

Birthplace of Thomas De Quincey

Thomas De Quincey (1785 – 1859) was a prolific writer in a variety of fields that varied from economics to fiction.

He is though, best known for his book, *Confessions of an English Opium Eater,* published in 1821: it has never been out of print since. By writing this book De Quincey is said to have invented recreational drug taking. Like much of his work *Confessions* is difficult to classify. It is seemingly a hybrid work which is a cross between his autobiographical experience as a laudanum addict and also his evaluation of the effects of the drug. When it first came out it scandalised English middle-class society.

As soon as it was published *Confessions* ... was criticized for its positive presentation of De Quincey's experience.

Although not readily associated with Manchester De Quincey was actually born here on August 15, 1785, at 86, Cross St, in the city centre. His father was a successful merchant with an interest in literature. De Quincey was also educated in Manchester and he wrote of it.

"Gloomy the streets of Manchester were at that time, mud below, smoke above."

His literary output was prolific and was widely read in England, USA and across Europe. When his collected works were issued in the 1850s in Boston, Massachusetts, they ran to 22 volumes. He is thought to have exerted literary influence over such writers as Edgar Allan Poe and the French poet Charles Baudelaire. By the age of 15, De Quincey was fluent in several languages including Ancient Greek.

Despite receiving a private education and his family's apparent wealth, at the age of 16, he fled Manchester Grammar School, citing *boredom* and proceeded to live the life of a penniless nomad, sleeping rough on the streets of Chester and Wales and mixing with drunkards and prostitutes. Eventually he was rehabilitated with his family.

He was well known to the leading Romantic poets such as William Wordsworth and Samuel Taylor Coleridge. For a time he lived with Wordsworth and his sister Dorothy at Dove Cottage, Grasmere, in the Lake District. He actually stayed on there when William moved into bigger premises to accommodate his growing family. Eventually though De Quincey would fall out of favour with Dorothy Wordsworth as he did with most people with whom he had any kind of relationship. These fallouts were usually connected one way or another to his conduct whilst under the influence of his addiction. In Dorothy's case, she took exception to his act of cutting the flowers down outside the windows of the cottage. Something that he said he needed to do to *let more light in*.

Eventually he married and fathered 8 children but he led a chaotic life moving from one address to another, usually to escape from or at least juggle his creditors. Throughout his life he continued to write and he produced many original works. He eventually settled in Edinburgh, where he died in considerably reduced circumstances to the ones that he had been born into. His life throughout, like many of his contemporaries, was marred by premature death, first of his siblings and latterly of his children. Many consider these deaths influenced his prose.

St Ann's Church

Consecrated in 1712 when Manchester was little more than a village containing fields and timber framed houses. St Ann's Church is a Grade 1 listed building and is the second oldest church in Manchester.

When Manchester was being developed, the datum for measuring and levelling was engraved into the corner of the building and can still be seen clearly today.

Engraved Datum in Church Wall.

Charles White (1728-1813)

Born in Manchester, himself the son of a surgeon, after studying medicine in London and Edinburgh he joined his father's practice in Manchester. From the onset he was recognised as an able and innovative surgeon. He was seen as a pioneer in the repair of fractured and broken bones and was also highly regarded in the field of obstetrics.

His views though on childbirth were controversial, as were his views on race and gender and almost certainly by today's standards he would have been considered a racist and a sexist.

In 1752, he co-founded the Manchester Royal Infirmary and was an honorary surgeon there until 1790. It is though, for none of these achievements or even his controversial views that he is best remembered, but for the case of the *Manchester Mummy*.

Around 1750, there was an upsurge in peoples minds in relation to the fear of being mistakenly buried alive. White was attending the funeral of wealthy John Beswick when it was brought to his attention that the *corpse's eyes had flickered*. White examined the body and certified it to be alive.

In fact John Beswick regained consciousness three days later and went on to live for many years after that. The incident so terrorised Beswick's witnessing and equally wealthy sister that she allegedly offered a large amount of money to Doctor White on the condition that after she died, her body be kept above ground and checked regularly for any signs of life. When she died in 1758, White himself embalmed her and had her stored away in an old clock case in his house until his own death in 1813. He did though allow viewings and a young Thomas De Quincey was one of those who actually went to see her at White's house. She became quite a celebrity of the day and was known colloquially as "The Manchester Mummy."

Tib Street Horn

This piece was commissioned to stand as a gateway to Manchester's 'Northern Quarter' and to represent the area's creativity. An idiosyncratic piece of art which is not easy to interpret. At the risk of sounding pretentious, it is probably whatever you want it to be. It was produced by Cornwall based artist David Kemp and placed in 1999. It appears as a serpent like figure which is coiled around the ruins of an old Victorian hat factory. Some commentators have likened it to a hybrid that is part saxophone and part crocodile although the artist himself has said that it is neither.

The Woolworth's Fire

This building which is still on the corner of Piccadilly and Oldham Street is currently being used by a variety of occupants for retail and leisure purposes. In 1979, the whole frontage was a store of F.W. Woolworth. It was claimed by Woolworth's to be their largest store in Europe, with six floors and two basement floors and had been on that site since 1929. The store was very popular with Mancunians, particularly the cafe. The whole store had no sprinkler system and for security reasons many of the windows above the ground floor were barred, the whole of the top floor windows were barred.

On Tuesday, 8th of May that year, at around 1:15pm, taxi driver John Featherstone was sitting in his cab which was parked outside the store in the taxi-rank. He was having his lunch. He would later infamously say that he '....Always had the same lunch on a Tuesday, two boiled eggs and a couple of Park Drive cigarettes.'

When he looked up, he saw smoke billowing from a third floor window and he raised the alarm. The record shows that the Fire Brigade received the call at 13:28 hours. In the next two minutes 12 alert calls were received but not one of them were from inside the building. There were at that time around 500 people inside the store.

Firefighters were at the scene in minutes. All together 150 fire fighters with 26 appliances attended the blaze. At 15:51 the fire was pronounced as 'surrounded.'

In that time though: 6 Firemen had been injured, 28 people had been rescued, 47 people were hospitalised and 10 people were dead.

After investigation it was found that the cause of the fire was a damaged electric cable which had mattresses and furniture stacked on top of it. People hadn't so much burnt to death but choked to death on the toxic fumes from the burning mattresses. It was the worst disaster to visit the city since World War 2. As a consequence of the Woolworth's fire, international laws regarding sprinkler systems, fire safety and furniture composition were changed.

Mother Mac's Pub

Mother Mac's Pub which stands almost completely alone at the junction of Back Piccadilly and Little Lever Street, is one of the oldest surviving pubs in Manchester. For the first one hundred and fifty years of its life, this pub was known as *The Wellington Inn*, but in the early 1970s it was re-named *Mother Mac's* and it is from this name that its fame and notoriety comes.

There are really two stories concerning this pub, the first story being as full of light and hope as the second is full of darkness and despair. Apart from the pub itself these stories have absolutely nothing in common and the characters in each one of them are as different as sunshine and cloud, but each story has become as enshrined in Mancunian folklore as the other. In chronological order these two stories are as follows.

After World War 2 a demobbed Irish Guardsman by the name of McClellan, who was himself an Irishman, took over the running of the *Wellington Inn*, in Back Piccadilly. A few years later, the exact date being elusive, he subsequently died and its management was left to his then widow Norah McClellan. Mrs McLellan, an Irishwoman, was allegedly slight in physical stature but was gifted with the twin assets for the management of such an establishment, of both a fiery Irish temper and immeasurable charm, and despite the fact that some of the toughest and most difficult men (and women) patronised the pub. There was no situation within its walls that Mrs McClellan ever failed to master. It was said that throughout her whole tenancy, which was right the way through to the late 1960s she didn't once resort to calling for back-up of any kind. Any disputes, no matter what their cause were resolved by her, there and then, on the premises. This style of management won her the respect of both the law and the lawless alike. There are many descriptions of how Mrs McClellan managed The Wellington Inn and one often referred to is, 'She ran it with firm kindness.' She was also known to lend a discreet helping hand to someone down on their luck and as she became established, she became known as Mother Mac and the pub itself gradually became an institution and in turn became known in Manchester as *Mother Mac's*. When she died in 1968, at the age of seventy three, she was so famous and respected throughout Manchester that her funeral brought the city to a standstill as thousands lined the streets to pay their respects. After her death the brewery officially re-named the pub *Mother Mac's*.

The death of Nora McClellan was not to be the final chapter in the prominence of Mother Mac's, although the next time this little back street boozer would come to public attention would be for both notorious and tragic reasons.

In the summer of 1976, with the Irish Landlady long dead but not forgotten, the pub found itself under new management, that of 30 years old Arthur Bradbury. His tenancy brought about an entirely different turn of events than Mother Mac's had seen under the stewardship of the cherished Mrs McClellan.

On June 17th, 1976, The Manchester Fire Brigade were alerted to a situation on the premises and two fire crews raced to the scene from nearby Whitworth Street.

Upon arrival a few minutes later they found the building locked up and ablaze. After bringing the fire under control, they forced entry into the premises and found before them a shocking sight. Inside were six badly burned corpses, three adults and three children, Arthur Bradbury was amongst them, the others were his wife, his three young children and his cleaning lady. The bodies were so badly burnt that formal identification could only be managed by dental records. After the appropriate official, statutory enquiries had taken place. The held view was that Arthur Bradbury had murdered his wife, his children and his cleaning lady. He then set the fire which he fell victim to himself.

More than 40 years later, Mother Mac's is now and has been for many years a popular destination pub which is completely safe and apart from a little jocular carousing on a Saturday- night, is incident free. There are those amongst us who could be forgiven for thinking that the ghost of Arthur Bradbury has been exorcised and the firm but kindly spirit of Mrs McClellan has returned.

The
Red Hat
Guide to MANCHESTER
CITY CENTRE

Lightning Source UK Ltd.
Milton Keynes UK
UKHW020448130819
347820UK00009B/78/P

9 781781 489468